BLUE PETER SPECIAL ASSIGNMENT

Isle of Skye, Isle of Man
Isle of Wight

EDWARD BARNES and DOROTHY SMITH

With full colour photographs
and with line drawings by Tony Morris

D1448509

BRITISH BROADCASTING CORPORATION

Blue Peter Special Assignment

THE ISLE OF SKYE	Film Cameramen	Alan Featherstone
		Keith Burton
		Martin Singleton
	Sound Recordists	Hugh Cleverly
		Alex Brown
	Director	Daniel Wolf
THE ISLE OF MAN	Film Cameramen	Ian Hilton
		Arthur Rowell
		John Else
		Julian Balchin
	Sound Recordists	Dick Manton
		Malcolm Bartram
		Ted Read
		Dennis Cartwright
	Director	David Brown
THE ISLE OF WIGHT	Film Cameramen	Phil Meheux
		Royston Halladay
	Film Recordists	Arthur Chesterman
		Roy Kendrick
	Director	Sarah Hellings
	Historical Research by	Dorothy Smith
	Research Assistant	Jane Tarleton
	Producer	Edward Barnes

Published by the British Broadcasting Corporation,
35 Marylebone High Street, London W1M 4AA

ISBN 0563 12841 0
First published 1975

© Edward Barnes and Dorothy Smith 1975

The illustration of Glenbrittle Youth Hostel is reproduced by kind permission
of the Scottish Youth Hostels Association
The Song of the Laxey Wheel © Stewart Slack
The photographs for this volume are by
Calum Neish (Isle of Skye), Peter Dobson (Isle of Man),
Joan Williams and Barry Boxall (Isle of Wight)

Printed in England
by Tinling (1973) Limited
(a member of the Oxley Printing Group)

Hello There!

This year's Blue Peter Special Assignments are about islands.

There's something romantic about the very word! It's an adventure to visit an island—and islands like to be visited. Islanders are proud individual people; they may welcome you to their shore, but you will always remain someone from the mainland. The Governor of the Isle of Wight, Earl Mountbatten of Burma, told me: "If you're not an islander, you're an overner. You may be a very pretty overner, but you're an overner for all that!"

These books are about five islands I've visited, from faraway exotic Hong Kong to the remote and beautiful Isle of Skye. They were all totally different from each other, yet they all had one thing in common; the islanders all believed *they* lived somewhere that was very special indeed.

Valerie Singleton

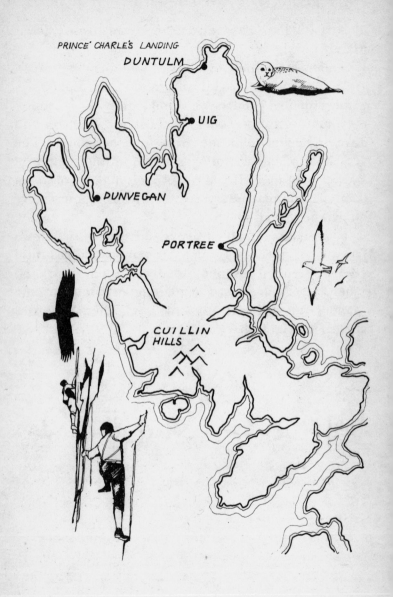

PRINCE CHARLES LANDING
DUNTULM
UIG
DUNVEGAN
PORTREE
CUILLIN HILLS

4

ISLE OF SKYE

The Misty Isle

At the very mention of the name Skye, everyone thinks of the Skye Boat song, and its haunting refrain

Carry the lad that's born to be king,
Over the sea to Skye.

I arrived one July day, by boat, to the actual stretch of coastline where Prince Charlie, the lad born to be king, was guided by Flora MacDonald, the island's heroine.

My mind was full of the song, and I was immediately captivated by the mysterious and beautiful island ahead of me.

Skye has been called "the Misty Isle". Under a bleak grey sky, the landscape is rugged and forbidding; then there is a gleam of sunshine, and everything is blue and green and shimmering silver.

I found it was easy to believe in all the myths of fairies and giants the people tell about the island. To the south are the Cuillin Mountains, snow-capped in winter and spring. The centre of the island is ribbed with lakes and streams and small lochs, typical Highland scenery. To the north it is the most rugged of all, stripped bare by the battering of the Atlantic weather.

The golden eagle is occasionally seen gliding over the jagged rocks, herons stand motionless on the banks of the lochs, and boatloads of tourists row out to watch the nurseries of baby seals on the tiny off-shore islets.

The Romans never came as far north as this, but there were other invaders. The Vikings swept down from the North Atlantic to the Skye coastline, and stayed for seven hundred years.

They ruled the island until 1263, when they were defeated by the Scottish clans at the battle of Largs.

The Cuillins

"The Cuillins are the most notable mountains in Britain, and have no equal in all the world" a Skye mountaineer has proudly proclaimed. Certainly the range of twenty pinnacles, each more than three thousand feet high, is a magnet drawing climbers, experts and beginners alike.

I too was fascinated by the peaks, misty grey or sombre black, looming over the green landscape, continually vanishing as the clouds swirled overhead, then suddenly appearing again.

Very much a beginner, I made my way to Glenbrittle Youth Hostel, which is the traditional base and starting place for climbers. The hostel stands alone, in the middle of nowhere, a stark functional building with dormitories for climbers, and a little house for Warden Bob Taplin, and his wife, baby and dogs.

I joined the other climbers of the day, and began to make ready. The right gear is important, for a climber's life may depend upon it. Warm clothes are essential, up on the bare mountain, so I piled on woollies, and jeans, and an anorak, and thick socks and climbing boots. The others—four young Scots on holiday from Perth, Clydeside, Wishart and Edinburgh, were more experienced than I was; they were going to do some rock climbing, so they were all equipped with tin helmets, to protect them from falling splinters of rock.

Glenbrittle Youth Hostel

I remembered a story I had been told about a mountaineer thirty years ago, who left Glenbrittle one June day, and returned exactly twenty-four hours later, having covered thirty miles, including climbing and descending the twenty peaks, and spending twelve and a half hours on the highest, most exposed ridge.

I didn't feel I was going to do anything like that today —I could far more easily believe the old legends, for long before the mountains were used for climbing, the people who lived on the island spoke of them with superstitious awe.

For years, they said, no living thing dwelt in the hills, then came Skiach, a great warrior goddess, and warriors and heroes from far and near followed, to consult her and learn from her.

At last the greatest hero of all, Cuchulin, arrived from Ireland, to challenge the warrior goddess to single combat. Skiach and Cuchulin fought together hour after hour, but neither was victorious.

Then Skiach's young daughter prepared a meal of milk and cheese, and called to them both to stop fighting, and to eat. But they would not stop, and fought on, on the mountains, and on the moors, and by the sea.

Then the girl roasted a deer, and again begged them to stop fighting, and to eat, but still the battle raged, though the smell of the roast meat was very tempting.

Then Skiach's daughter roasted another deer, and stuffed it with hazelnuts, which were supposed to bring wisdom and knowledge, and once more she called to the warriors to eat. This time they smelt the hazelnuts of wisdom, as well as the roast meat.

Skiach thought: "The hazelnuts of wisdom will teach me how to defeat Cuchulin." And Cuchulin thought: "The hazelnuts of wisdom will teach me how to defeat Skiach." So they stopped fighting, and they sat down together to eat.

And the hazelnuts indeed brought wisdom, and they each realised that neither of them could ever win the battle, or defeat the other.

So Skiach and Cuchulin made peace, and promised if either was attacked by anyone else, the other would come to help. And Skiach called the hills where they had fought Cuillin Hills, after the hero, and the island was called Skye, after the warrior goddess.

And here I was, on Skiach's island, ready to climb Cuchulin's Hills, under the leadership of Warden Bob Taplin. He began by looking at the Blue Peter crew, dressed as mountaineers, but laden with film cameras, spare cameras, rolls of film, and all the bag and baggage of a film crew at work.

"You can't carry all that," he said firmly. "We'll share it out amongst us." So the young Scots climbers kindly helped to hump the gear, and the climb began.

But although Glenbrittle is the base for climbers, it is a long way from the real high peaks, and first of all we had to cross a stretch of rough heathland, where even the sheep never came, and where outcrops of rock appeared through the scrubby grass. Even these lower slopes were steep, and boggy with the streams pouring down continually from the mountainsides—at one point a waterfall splashed and gurgled into the glen below us. There was no apparent path; there was gorse, bracken, and tangled roots of heather. It was rugged and beautiful, and it seemed to stretch for *miles*. I stopped to get my breath, and looked down at the lovely view below. Then I turned to look up at the beckoning peaks—and they had entirely disappeared! A mist had fallen, shutting out the way ahead.

"It's worth going on," said Bob Taplin. "The mist will probably clear before we start climbing." So we struggled on, and I wondered what it would be like when "climbing" started.

Hours later, Bob called us to a halt. We stopped abruptly—the mist was thinner, and there seemed to be an empty space in front of us. As we peered, we saw it was a little loch—a pool set high up in the hills. It was absolutely still, and rather uncanny. Bob suggested lunch, so we began unpacking.

"How are we doing?" I asked.

"Well, we've taken four hours so far. Usually we do this stretch in an hour and a half. It's the mist, and all the gear we're carrying."

He did not sound a bit reproachful, but I looked at the Blue Peter crew, and they looked at me.

"Look," said Director Daniel Wolf, "we don't want

to spoil your day. We can't do much filming in the mist. You go on, and we'll go slowly back."

"Would you mind?" asked the young man from Edinburgh. "You'll miss the climbing."

"You go right ahead," I said. "Never mind us!"

They got up eagerly, and we watched them vanish round a turn of the hills. More slowly, we gathered ourselves together, and began the long tramp home.

Even if we couldn't call ourselves mountaineers, the day had given us a great respect for the Cuillin Hills, and the mountaineers who climb them.

One Man and his Dogs

It is almost impossible to persuade anything to grow on the bare lower slopes of the hills. There are three hundred thousand acres of farming land on Skye, but only two thousand acres actually produce any crops.

So the people keep cows, and sheep. Two hundred and seventy-five thousand acres are used for rough grazing by sheep and cattle farmers, and, although there are only seven thousand people living on the whole Isle of Skye, there are more than a hundred thousand sheep. They roam the steep hillsides in search of scanty pasture, scattering so far that it is difficult to see them all, let alone look after them. The sheep farmers rely tremendously on their dogs, as I found, when I went to see Mr Calum MacLeod on his farm just a few miles outside Portree.

It was pouring with rain when we arrived at Mr MacLeod's farm—though farm is rather a grand word for it, because it consists of two tiny wooden huts on the roadside, at the foot of the rolling hills where over a thousand acres Mr MacLeod runs four hundred sheep. We got in touch with him first of all by leaving a note nailed to the door of the empty hut, asking him to phone us at our hotel—it would have taken the whole day to find him! But today he came striding through the mist over the brow of the hill to meet us, wielding an impressive crook, with a thistlehead handle carved from a whole sheep's horn.

He was a tall, attractive, splendidly upright man, with kind eyes and a neat moustache.

"I'm afraid you're a wee bit unlucky with the weather —and so am I, because I'd hoped to get a lot of shearing done today."

I began to climb the hill beside him, as his three dogs trickled along at his heels. On the crest of the hill we looked down into the valley where a flock of sheep were grazing, about a mile away from us.

"Now I've got to get these sheep up here into that pen," he said, indicating a small square area of fencing, with a gate opening into it. "And then I'm going to shear them."

"How long would it take you without dogs?" I asked.

He laughed. "I've no idea, but single-handed I'd have to catch them and then carry them back one at a time, so it would take me the best part of a week."

The dogs had seen the sheep, and they froze in their tracks; one of them had his right foot raised, as if turned to stone.

"Away you go," Mr MacLeod said, in a soft conversational tone, and all three dogs streaked away. They reached the flock in seconds, Rock making a wide circle to get ahead of the sheep and cut off their retreat, whilst Tweed and Lass went to the left and right.

Mr MacLeod gave a shrill piercing whistle, and all three dogs dropped to the ground as if they had been shot, Tweed skidding about six feet on his front over the short wet grass. The sheep bunched together, and then, as if operated by clockwork, they all turned at the same time and began to come back towards us.

The concentration of every dog was total. Their eyes never left the sheep for an instant, their ears cocked waiting for the next command.

"Come bye, Tweed. Away to me, Lass. Lie down, Rock."

I asked the sheep-farmer what "Come bye" meant.

"'Come bye' means come round to the left, and 'Come away to me' means come round to your right. When they are too far off to hear that, we translate the commands into whistles, because they have acute hearing, and whistles travel a long way over the hills."

While he was talking, one of the sheep made a dash for freedom, but Tweed was after it in a flash, gently, silently and firmly pushing it back into the flock.

"You didn't have to tell him to do that," I said, surprised.

"Aye, well, they have a good idea what's wanted of them. After all, they do it every day!" he said, drily.

By now the sheep were quite close to us, zigzagging their way towards the pen. The whistles had stopped, and the shouts became softly-spoken words, punctuated by a sudden rapped command.

"Away, Lass, lie down, Rock. Come bye Tweed. Come on, Rock!"

Then Mr MacLeod casually opened the gate of the pen, and with a gracious sweep of his crook ushered in the entire flock.

The whole operation had taken less than fifteen minutes.

The Crofters

Only in the last fifty years have conditions changed much on Skye; before that the ordinary folk, the crofters, had lived in much the same way for hundreds of years.

It was a terribly hard life, with the crofters and their families always on the brink of destitution. They lived in small communities, growing hardy crops like turnips and potatoes, milking a cow and perhaps turning their hand to fishing from time to time.

There was no coal and little timber on the island, so for fuel they used peat, which is dried out turf from bogs, held together by a tangle of heather and bracken roots. It has to be cut out of the bog in blocks, like the turf for a lawn, then it is arranged in piles to dry, and later carried back home to the croft. Peat is still used on the island, and I was curious about the black squares, arranged carefully on the hillside, until I knew what they were.

Even after it's been stacked out all summer, the peat is not quite dry, and when it is burnt it gives off a lot of smoke and smell, and not much light and heat.

A croft has been preserved, just as it was eighty years ago, when people stopped living there. It stands in a beautiful position, overlooking Loch Dunvegan. It looked picturesque and pretty with its rough thatched roof, but once inside, I could hardly see anything at first, because of the smoke from the peat fire, burning on a hearth in the middle of the room.

Cutting peat

As I got used to it, I looked around. It was very small—it was hard to imagine a family of twelve living in the cramped dark room, but this often happened. They cooked all their food—mostly potatoes and oatmeal porridge—on the fire.

Apart from the main room, there was just one other, right next to it, where the family kept their cows, if they were lucky enough to have any, and even a few sheep, in the worst of the bitter winter.

No wonder, living this bleak hard life, that few of the crofters reached old age!

In the middle of the eighteenth century, two hundred years ago, there were eleven thousand people living on Skye, many of them struggling along in crofts like the one I saw. A hundred years later, the population had doubled, and there were twenty-three thousand islanders.

Then disaster struck. Sheep farming was introduced, and the Lords and clan chieftains realised there would be a great deal more grazing land for the sheep, if they could thin out the population.

These disastrous moves were called "land clearances": crofters were forced off the land in their thousands; some moved to the mainland, many emigrated, some died of destitution. By 1883 the population of the island was down to seventeen thousand: now it is only seven thousand.

Like the rest of the Highlands, Skye has never recovered from the notorious land clearances. That is why, wherever you drive on the island you see piles of stones, tumble-down walls, all that remains of hundreds of deserted, ruined crofts.

Crofts aren't the only ruins I found on the island. For five hundred years, the history of Skye was the history of two warring clans, the MacLeods and the MacDonalds. It is sad, looking over the calm beauty of the empty landscape, to realise that its scattered inhabitants were locked in bitter conflict, but that is how it was.

Duntulm Castle, the fortress on the promontory, was the stronghold of the MacDonalds. It is in ruins now, but the walls still tower over the cliffs, and you can see what an impressive building it was. The castle is over a thousand years old; before the MacDonalds came it was first a Celtic, then a Norse, stronghold. To the south, you can still see a natural oval mound; this was called Moot Hill, and it was where the Lord dispensed justice to his clansmen.

One window, with a magnificent view facing north towards the Hebrides, was called the Piper's Window, and there is a sad story about it. Tradition says that once, near the beginning of the eighteenth century, the nurse of the young heir of the MacDonalds stood by this window singing, the baby in her arms. Suddenly, he fell, down onto the cruel rocks below, and was killed. Soon afterwards the MacDonalds left their unhappy castle to fall into ruins, and moved to their present castle of Armadale in the south of the island.

The MacLeods, on the other hand, have not moved. Their castle, Dunvegan, is not ruined, and is still the home and headquarters of the clan's leader, the MacLeod of MacLeod, as it has been for seven hundred years, the only castle lived in by the same family for so long in all Scotland.

The castle dominates Dunvegan Bay, and was doubly strong against attack, because it had no gateway on the landward side. The only entrance was from the sea. Members of the family and friendly guests arrived by boat, and made their way up through a gate to the castle. Strangers were not encouraged, and the MacDonalds never got through the castle's defences.

The endless battles and skirmishes fought outside were savage and merciless. Prisoners captured in the fighting were dragged back to the castle, and thrown into the dungeon.

"Thrown" means exactly that—they were tossed through a trapdoor, probably breaking their arms or legs in the fall. Once down there, they were left to die, of exposure or starvation, tormented by the smells of cooking from the castle kitchens which wafted to them through a grating set in their gloomy cell.

The fighting days have long been over; the MacLeods and MacDonalds were united by marriage two hundred years ago, and today a great door on the landward side welcomes the visitors who go to Dunvegan Castle every year.

The Fairy Flag

The MacDonalds were fortunate in all their early battles, they claim, because for centuries they were helped by even earlier inhabitants of Skye—the little folk—the People of the Hills—the Fairies.

Centuries ago, the story goes, Ian, the fourth Chief of the MacLeods, married a fairy bride. They lived together very happily, and had a baby son, until one

17

The castle of Dunvegan

day she had a call from her own people, that she must go back to them.

Sadly her husband took her to a bridge crossing a stream gushing down the mountainside—it is called the Fairy Bridge to this day. As they said goodbye, she put a square of the softest, finest silk into his hands.

"This is a Fairy Flag," she said. "Your people may wave it when they are hard pressed in battle, and my people will come to save your clan. But you must wave it only three times—after that all the magic will have gone."

Then she vanished, and Ian never saw her again.

The Fairy Flag has been waved only twice by the MacLeods, and the second and last time was four hundred years ago, in a village ten miles from Dunvegan Castle.

Trumpan Church is a ruin now, but then, one misty Sunday morning in May, it was thronged with the MacLeods who lived close by, who were attending a service. Silently, eight boatloads of MacDonalds landed on the beach nearby, surrounded the thatched church, and set it on fire.

Just one woman escaped from the flames, badly hurt. She found a young boy, and told him to gather what help he could from the village.

From Dunvegan Castle the look-out had seen the flames; the garrison seized the Fairy Flag, and rushed to the relief of Trumpan.

They found that the handful of people the boy had gathered together had delayed the MacDonalds, who had not been able to get away. The tide had turned, their boats were high and dry on the beach— and the MacLeods were advancing to give battle!

It was a terrible struggle, with no end in sight, for both sides were desperate. At last, the MacLeods felt they had no choice, and waved the Fairy Flag. Immediately the MacLeods took fresh heart, and the spirit went out of the MacDonalds, who thought a great new army was advancing upon them.

The MacLeods were soon victorious, and the bodies of friend and foe alike were buried together under the dyke alongside the sea.

The Fairy Flag has never been waved since that day. It is kept in Dunvegan Castle, carefully preserved under glass. It just looks like a faded, tattered, scrap of silk, and it is hard to believe that it still holds its ancient power.

But the MacLeods think it still has the power to protect them in danger, and that, if the need arises, it can still be used to save the clan.

The MacLeod of MacLeod

No one is more sure of the power of the Fairy Flag than the present MacLeod of MacLeod—the twenty-eighth chieftain of the clan, Dame Flora MacLeod.

The chieftain of the Clan MacLeod has lived in Dunvegan Castle for six hundred and fifty years. Today it is the home of Dame Flora MacLeod, the only woman ever to bear the title, and the undisputed first lady of Skye.

She is ninety-six years old, with the energy of someone half her years, and she is the greatest authority on the long and turbulent history of her family.

I was honoured to be received by her in the great drawing-room at Dunvegan Castle.

She sat, a tiny figure, in a large arm-chair surrounded by huge portraits of past chieftains, including one of herself wearing the tartan of the MacLeods. The room, Dame Flora told me, was not always an elegant drawing-room, but was for centuries the Great Hall, where the clan lived and ate. It was a fortress within a fortress, with a single narrow entrance and a nine-foot-thick wall of rock that was never penetrated by an invader.

Today MacLeods are everywhere in the world, and every year hundreds of them come to Dunvegan on a pilgrimage to the land of their ancestors.

I asked Dame Flora about how many MacLeods there were altogether.

"Americans always ask me that," she replied. "I always tell them 'Go and look in the telephone book of your own city, and when you've counted the MacLeods there, you can start to multiply the answer with the rest of the cities of the world!'"

Then, in the same matter-of-fact voice, turning to me she said, "Now I'd like to tell your viewers something about the fairies, because they've been very good to my family for the last six hundred years."

I looked in the brilliant blue eyes for the hint of a twinkle, but she was utterly serious.

"You see that frame by the window—there is the Fairy Flag of the MacLeods."

I looked at the tattered, faded piece of cloth in its austere black frame. It seemed incredible that the dull-looking object had twice led the MacLeods to victory against seemingly invincible odds, and it was harder still to believe that it came originally from some strange land inhabited entirely by fairies.

"Is it true that it can only be waved one more time, and then all the magic is gone?" I asked.

"Well, that's always been said, and I believe it's absolutely true. Mind you, if anyone took it out of that case now, I think it would crumble to dust, so it must be true that it would perish completely if it were waved again."

Dame Flora went on to tell me that although the Fairy Flag had only been actually waved twice, it had been carried into battle, furled, on several occasions, as an inspiration to the fighting MacLeods.

"Even as recently as the last war, MacLeods from all over the world came here to take photographs of the Flag, to carry with them into battle."

Plucking up all my courage, I asked her if she herself really believed in fairies.

Dame Flora MacLeod of MacLeod, twenty-eighth Chieftain of the Clan MacLeod, smiled and said: "They asked my small great-grandson, Patrick Adam, that question."

There was a silence—then I asked her what Patrick Adam had replied.

"He turned to them and said: 'Of course I believe in fairies—I'm descended from one!'"

Piping and Gaelic are on the Timetable

Every Midsummer, on 22 June, Dame Flora and some of the closest friends of her family travel across the waters of Dunvegan Bay, to land at a scattered village called Boreraig.

They are escorted by the finest bagpipers in Scotland, who play throughout the journey. When they arrive,

22

everyone climbs the hill, and an old ceremony takes place. The piper of the MacLeods gives a penny to the holder of the land. Once an old piping school stood on this place, and pipers from all over Scotland came to perfect their art. Now the school is in ruins, but the MacLeods still pay rent for the site, and then a lament is played, by the cairn of stones which commemorates the famous school of the MacLeod pipers.

Though the ancient school of piping is no more, piping is still taught throughout the Isle of Skye. Farquhar MacIntosh is the Piping Instructor to four schools on the island, and he drives round from one school to the other just like any other visiting master, with the bagpipes on the back seat of his car.

Skye was the first place to have piping instruction in schools, though it is now taught all over Scotland.

I wanted to find out more about this very unusual school subject, so Farquhar took me to Dunvegan School, where there are only sixty-one children, but almost all of them are learning the pipes. It's a difficult instrument, and before you start with the actual pipes, you play on something called a chanter, which is a mouthpiece, and a pipe that gives you practice in fingering. The distinctive bagpipe sound comes later on, when the windbags are added.

When I went into the classroom, I found it was very like a recorder lesson in an English school, except the sound was totally different, and the chanter is much more difficult to play.

Although people always think of men as pipers, I was delighted to find that some of the best chanter players at Dunvegan School are girls, like sixteen-year-old Myra McNab, but it was a different story when they came to the actual bagpipes.

"I tried and tried," said Myra, "but I didn't seem to have enough puff."

I sympathised, remembering the time that I'd had a go, when I was doing Blue Peter Special Assignment Edinburgh. After five minutes of puffing and blowing I only succeeded in making a very rude noise.

"It's a strange thing," said Farquhar, "that when they start on the chanter the girls come on far better than the boys, but when it comes to the actual pipes the girls seem to give up easier. Although," he added hastily, "we have some excellent girl pipers in Scotland today!"

In the same school, there was another rather special class—they were learning Gaelic, the old traditional language of the island. There was a time, not so long ago, when a boy heard speaking Gaelic at school might be strapped for it. The parents did not object, because they knew that if you wanted to make your way on the mainland you had to speak English.

Now all that has changed. In 1959 a law was passed that made the teaching of Gaelic compulsory in Highland schools. Not many children learn it from their parents any more, but some learn to speak it fluently at school.

Mrs MacKenzie's class of eight-year-olds was singing a song in Gaelic when I arrived. When they had finished, I asked them if they found the Gaelic language difficult to learn. Most of them said they found it pretty hard, because nowadays they could hear very little Gaelic spoken outside school.

Yet every so often, Mrs MacKenzie told me, a child will come down from a croft in the most remote part,

and arrive at school not speaking a word of English. Gaelic is the only language they have ever heard spoken.

There are still Highland poets who write modern poems in the Gaelic. Mrs MacKenzie asked her best pupil, seven-year-old Shona MacDonald, to come out in front of the class, to recite a poem written by a local bard who had died only recently.

Shona stood up confidently, and I listened to the soft musical sounds, not able to understand a word, but Mrs MacKenzie had told me what the poem was all about.

An old man was talking about Skye, seventy years ago. Then, he says, children walked to school, ten miles, barefoot, carrying a block of peat under their arm every day—their contribution to the school heating.

But today, he says scornfully, the children are driven to school, and their teachers say to them: "Take care the wind doesn't blow too hard on you!"

Shona acted the old man's scorn in the last verse very well, but as I looked round the room of the little Gaelic speakers, and heard the wail of Mr MacIntosh's pipe class from across the passage, I thought the young people of Skye have a great deal to be proud of, in the way they are keeping the old traditions alive.

The Old Songs of Skye

Miss Betsy MacLeod is the mainspring of a group of eight ladies, who sit together and sing the songs traditionally sung by the women who wove the beautiful native tweed cloth, years ago. These songs are called "waulking" songs and used to be sung when the tweed was being shrunk into its final shape. The ladies sat round the table, beating the tweed with their hands and singing such songs as *Lassie of the brown hair* and *Ho my sweetheart* and one of the songs for folding up the completed web of tweed called *My plaid is wet*— which in that climate, must happen often! They told me there were songs with the right rhythm for all the household chores, like making butter, milking, and spinning—a highland version of Music While you Work!

On Skye, the name for a traditional social evening is a ceilidh—which is pronounced "caley".

I went to hear the songs sung at these evenings, and I found that here, too, many people on Skye were determined to keep the old traditions alive.

Jonathan MacDonald is an expert in the old Gaelic ways, and his sister is renowned all over the island for her singing. They explained the strange haunting quality I found in all the music.

The songs I heard date back to the most important event that ever happened on Skye, the escape of Prince Charles Stuart—Bonnie Prince Charlie—from the mainland in 1746. After he left for France, the English systematically tried to stamp out the old Scotland. All the bagpipes were destroyed, and it was death to try to keep them, because the redcoat soldiers might kill you if bagpipes were found in your possession.

So the only way of keeping the bagpipe music alive was by singing it—mouth music, it was called. The songs became a form of music in its own right; the words are Gaelic, but the sound is like pipe music.

Bonnie Prince Charlie and Flora MacDonald

In Dunvegan Castle there are many reminders of that rebellion in 1745, and of Skye's great heroine, Flora MacDonald. They keep her picture—her shoes—even part of her stays!

And there is another important link with the '45.

The King in London was George II, a German, who knew nothing about Britain. Many people in England, and even more in Scotland, thought he had no right to be King. So when they drank to the King's health, they passed their wine glasses over a bowl of water, and drank to the King "over the water"—the man they thought should be King, James Stuart, who had been driven out of the country, and now lived far away across the sea. One of those glasses is kept in Dunvegan.

The most precious relic of all is a lock of hair, cut from the head of James Stuart's son—the handsome much-loved Prince Charles Edward. Bonnie Prince Charlie has been the theme of pictures, songs and stories for more than two hundred years.

In 1745 the Prince went to Scotland in a gallant attempt to win back the country for his father. He landed without an army, on a deserted shore.

"Go home, laddie," one Scotsman advised him. "I have come home," said the Prince firmly, and soon chieftains and clansmen flocked to his standard.

He entered Edinburgh in joyful triumph, and ruled at Holyrood House for one brief year—Charlie's year, they called it.

But the daydreams ended with the nightmare battle of Culloden. In less than an hour, the English redcoats cut the Highlanders to pieces, while Charles, almost in tears, looked on helpless. Then the army, under their leader, "Butcher" Cumberland, laid waste the countryside, killing, looting, burning, and reducing the Highlands to despair and ruin.

Charles was a wanted man now, under sentence of death. There was a price on his head—£30,000—almost £1,000,000 in today's money. Charlie's year was over, and he was on the run. He took to the heather.

He managed to make his way across Scotland to the coast, hoping to get a boat that would take him to France. He reached the Outer Isles, beyond Skye, but no boat came, and the hunt was getting close.

For ten weeks, he trudged miles, hiding in caves and drinking from springs, with one or two companions. It was death to help him, and the reward for betraying him was beyond belief, and everywhere English troops on the look-out combed the countryside.

Yet everywhere someone was ready to help him, and set him a few miles further on his way. At the end of June, in South Uist, he determined to get back to the mainland, by way of Skye.

That is how he came to meet Flora MacDonald.

She was related to the MacDonald chieftains of Skye; her family supported the Prince, and many of the clan had fallen at Culloden. She was visiting her brother on South Uist, where he was a farmer. Her stepfather was on the island too, in charge of the local militia, but Prince Charles' supporters believed he would go some way to help them. So they went to Flora, in the fields where she was helping with the cattle.

She was brought to the exhausted Prince, and they begged her to help. At first she was unwilling, because she did not want to make trouble for her family, but soon she had made a plan.

She went to her stepfather, and he, carefully asking no questions, gave her a permit to cross from South Uist to Skye, with one manservant, and an Irish maid called Betty Burke. Then she gathered some clothes that would fit her tall new maid, and took them to the Prince.

Soon Betty Burke was ready, in calico gown and petticoats, shawl, and lace cap. The Prince hated the cap, and he kept getting angry and making jokes about it.

Flora was a reserved, serious girl, and she was fascinated by the gay light-hearted manner the Prince kept through all his troubles. He was very considerate and respectful to Flora—he referred to her as The Lady, and always called her Miss—but sometimes he joked with her.

He wanted to keep a pistol at his waist, under the petticoats, but Flora would not allow it. "It will give you away, if the soldiers search you," she insisted.

"Indeed Miss," said the Prince, "if they search me that closely they will surely discover me anyway!"

Flora MacDonald took the Prince and a companion down to the shore. A boat was waiting, with four rowers and a pilot, and they set out, over the sea to Skye, running the risk of sudden storms, or attacks from soldiers. They rowed all night, until next morning they were close to the coast of Skye.

The isles have scarcely changed in the two hundred and thirty years since that June day, and it is possible to follow almost exactly in their footsteps.

As the boat approached the coast, they were fired on by watchful troops.

"Don't be afraid, Miss," said the Prince. "We shall not be taken." But Flora was not afraid.

They landed on a little deserted beach, where a stream ran down to the sea. The Prince—dressed as Betty Burke—was persuaded to sit on a trunk by the stream, while Flora went ahead.

She walked over the fields by the path that led to Monkstad House, where she knew her aunt, Lady Margaret MacDonald, would help them.

The house is in ruins now but in those days it was a fine house. She approached carefully, and found the British Redcoat Officer was there!

She gave her aunt a hasty explanation, and then sat down with the officer in the dining-room. She showed him her permit to land with her maid, but she kept him talking so that he did not bother to go down to the beach to inspect the boat she had arrived in.

All the time, Flora kept looking into the garden, where her aunt was talking to a friend, MacDonald of Kingsburgh, and planning the next step. She saw him slip away, to fetch the Prince by a quiet road up from the beach, so then she told the officer that she must hurry away, to join her mother at home.

Flora met the rest of the party, and they moved off. They followed quiet roads, but it was Sunday evening, and they kept meeting people on their way home from church, who stared at the tall, uncouth, serving woman.

They had several streams to cross, and Flora scolded when the Prince hitched his skirts up above his knees. The Prince laughed, and thanked her—and next time he didn't pick them up high enough, so they trailed in the water.

At last they reached that night's stopping place—it

was called Kingsburgh House, the home of MacDonald of Kingsburgh. It was, for a brief while, safe and unsuspected, and the Prince was made welcome. MacDonald's wife apologised for the poor supper, but the Prince insisted they all sit down with him, and ate hungrily.

After supper, Mrs MacDonald asked if the Prince would give a keepsake to her and to Flora, and the Prince bent his head, while Flora cut a lock of his hair.

Quiet Flora would never have asked for it herself, but she was glad to have it, and treasured it all her life. That is the lock of hair now kept at Dunvegan Castle.

The Prince slept well that night, in a proper bed, with sheets. Next morning Mrs MacDonald folded the sheets carefully, while Flora helped the Prince to dress.

"Oh, Miss, you have forgotten my apron," he kept saying. "Don't forget it, it is the most important part of my dress!"

They left Kingsburgh House, which still stands and is occupied, and made their way to Portree, the tiny capital of the island, where a few friends waited for them. It was raining hard, and they were afraid the Prince would get wet, but he only said he was sorry "the Lady" should have been out in the rain—though Flora, Skye born and bred, probably hardly noticed the weather.

A boat was waiting, and the Prince changed into Highland dress. Then he said goodbye to Flora.

He kissed her, she used to recall. Then he said: "For all that has happened, I hope, Madam, we shall meet at the Court of St James's. I will reward you there for what you have done!"

But she never saw him again. With tears in her eyes

she watched as the boat taking him away grew fainter, while she prayed for his safety.

He reached Europe, three months later. She had indeed helped to save his life. But he never came back to Scotland again, and by the end of his life there was little left of the gaiety and gallantry that had carried Bonnie Prince Charlie through all his adventures.

Flora became a national heroine. She was arrested and imprisoned, but after two years she was set free, and returned to Skye.

She married the son of MacDonald of Kingsburgh, who was linked so closely with her great adventure.

At last she died, on Skye. Her body was wrapped in the sheets, so carefully preserved, that the Prince had slept in at Kingsburgh more than forty years before.

A mile-long procession followed her, and twelve pipers played a lament. Flora MacDonald was buried on a windy hill, looking out to the Western Isles.

On the great granite cross over her grave are the words: "She leaves a name that will be mentioned in history, and, where courage and fidelity be virtues, mentioned with honour."

Everyone loves the romantic story of Flora Mac-Donald and the Prince she helped to save. Yet she is a heroine amongst a people of heroes; for not all the people of Skye, nor all the people of Scotland, supported the Prince, but it is to their everlasting credit, and it is their eternal pride, that in spite of the king's ransom that was offered, not one Scotsman betrayed the Prince.

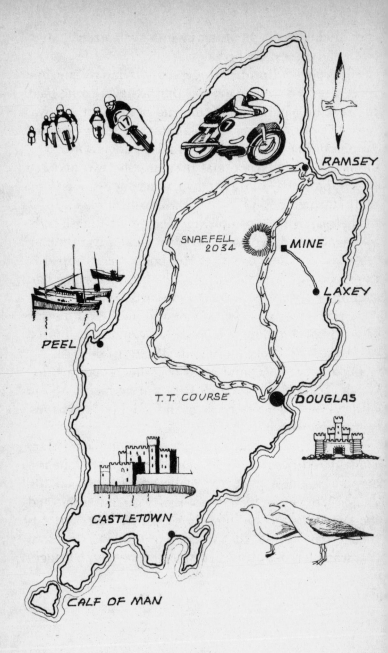

RAMSEY

SNAEFELL
2034

MINE

LAXEY

PEEL

T.T. COURSE

DOUGLAS

CASTLETOWN

CALF OF MAN

ISLE OF MAN

"Imports trippers . . ."

"The island imports trippers and exports kippers"—
that is how one guide book sums up the Isle of Man,
and as far as it goes it's true.

In the busy holiday season, eighty-seven boats a
week make the three-and-a-half-hour crossing from
Liverpool to Douglas, and on the June day I sailed out
from Liverpool, one particular kind of tripper was
being imported in large numbers. Everyone was
making for the world-famous T.T. motor-bike races.

My boat was the tenth to leave Liverpool in a very
hectic twenty-four hours, and it was still solid with
bikes and riders.

The steamers of the Isle of Man Steam Packet
Company have been the life-line of the island now for
a hundred and forty-five years, from the days of the
original paddle steamers, to the latest diesel ships
of today.

The approach to Douglas harbour has always been
rather tricky, so all the ships blow a prolonged blast on
the siren, to give warning of their approach. I was
allowed to give the warning on our ship, so I pulled the
cord, and with the blast in my ears, and the motor
cycles being swung up by crane, I looked out from the
noisy, busy ship to the quiet stretch of Douglas Bay.

Horse Trams

The T.T. racing is spread over a week, and I arrived a few days before the first event, so that I could see something of the island before the bikes took over.

I began by taking one of the oldest forms of Manx transport, the horse-drawn tram that runs right along the extensive promenade at Douglas. The horse trams date back to 1876, when Douglas was little more than a busy fishing town. Today it is the island's capital, and the biggest tourist resort, with all the bustle and excitement of the British seaside.

The horse plodded his way steadily in front of the line of tall, dazzlingly-painted boarding houses, the beach with its sunbathers and swimmers on the other side, and I asked Bob Moore, the placid bespectacled Manxman who was the conductor, about the service. My horse, he told me, was ten years old. The trip along the front takes twenty minutes, so each horse usually does four round trips, which takes just over two hours, and then he gets a three-hour rest. The effort comes when he has to get the tram started, but between the stops it runs easily along the metal rails.

I asked what happened when the horses got past working, and Mr Moore told me that the lucky ones are bought by a kind-hearted society, and go to a Home of Rest. In the winter they are cared for in the farm's stables, but in the summer they are free to wander round the surrounding fields—a well-earned retirement.

I went to see the forty-seven pensioners, who grazed on a gentle slope with a glorious view of the sea. They looked quiet, sleek, and contented, and I wondered if they knew that they had helped to provide the Isle of

Man with one of its star tourist attractions.

The horse-drawn trams aren't the only colourful means of transport on the island. A hundred-year-old steam railway runs from Douglas towards the south, and to the north, starting where the horse trams finish, is an electric tramway, which runs for sixteen miles up the eastern coast. This also dates from the last century.

The man behind this venture was a Scot, called Alexander Bruce. He realised that tourism was fast becoming the island's main industry so he planned the line for tourists. "We want plenty of bends," he told his engineer, "so that the view keeps changing!"—and plenty of bends he got.

The Laxey Wheel

It's quickly obvious to the visitor that tourism is the Isle of Man's chief industry today, but this hasn't always been so. In the last century the island made a great deal of money from its mines, for there were considerable deposits of lead, zinc and even silver in the Manx hills. There was no coal, though, and that is why the pumping engines for the mines were usually powered by water, not by steam.

One engineer had his eye on the tourist market at the same time as he considered the problems of the mines. His name was Roger Casement, and he worked for the lead mining company at Laxey, a small village eight miles north of Douglas. The company required a new water pump to keep the mines dry, so Casement's solution was to design a pump powered by a water wheel so spectacular that tourists would travel up the Laxey Valley from Douglas to see it.

The Laxey wheel

The Laxey Wheel, built in 1854, has a diameter of seventy-two feet. It took a thousand gallons of water a minute to keep it turning, and developed enough power to pump two hundred gallons of water a minute up from the workings. The beauty of it was that the power came from water that would otherwise have seeped down into the mine.

The pump, eight hundred yards up the valley from the wheel, no longer works, and the connecting rods that ran along the top of the viaduct have been lost, but when the hundred and sixty-eight buckets have filled up with water, the wheel still turns, and looks just as spectacular.

It is painted dramatically in crimson and black, and it soars up between the sloping green sides of the valley.

The towering metalwork makes a criss-cross pattern of shadows on the sunlit grass, and as the wheel turns the shadows move in a slow rythmical dance, so that the Laxey Wheel, designed a hundred and twenty years ago, looks like a brilliant and original fantasy by a modern artist.

A Manx song writer has summed up the chequered history of the Laxey Wheel in a song that is still popular on the island:

When Laxey was a mining village many years ago
There were six hundred miners working under Captain Rowe
But the bottom of the mine shaft was below the water line
So they had to build a wheel to pump the water from the mine.
And the Laxey Wheel keeps turning, turning, turning
In Lady Isabella's memory.
And while the water flows the Laxey Wheel still goes
And the Laxey River runs down to the sea.

It's stood now for a hundred years through wind, rain
* snow and drought*
And it will keep on turning till the sands of time run out
And though the main mine building is no more than a shell
The wheel still stands majestic in the shadow of Snaefell
And the Laxey Wheel keeps turning, turning, turning
In Lady Isabella's memory.
And while the water flows the Laxey Wheel still goes
And the Laxey River runs down to the sea.

The Mine Disaster

The Laxey Wheel cost a great deal of money to build, but it cost absolutely nothing to run, and it pumped away for seventy-five years; in fact, it was the mining company that ground to a halt first. The mine shafts had become too deep to be worked either profitably or safely, a fact that was high-lighted by a serious mining disaster in 1897.

It happened further up the Laxey Valley at the Snaefell Mine, in the shadow of the island's highest mountain.

There were just over forty miners working on the Snaefell shaft at that time, the whole operation being in charge of the Mine Captain, John Kewley. He was a veteran of more prosperous days, when the mine had been shallow and easy to work. Now it was a thousand feet deep, and although there was a small water-powered hoist to bring up the lead, the miners had to use a series of long ladders to get to the workings. It took twenty minutes to climb down, thirty-five to get back.

As the shift came to an end on Saturday, 8 May, two miners were half-way through the job of renewing old roof-timbers in a tunnel on the hundred-and-thirty-fathom level. They had worked by the light of half a dozen candles, and as they left to start the long climb up to the surface, they took care to extinguish them all.

But they were not careful enough. One candle continued to glow very faintly, perhaps for a matter of minutes, perhaps for an hour—and then suddenly, fanned by a chance gush of air, it burst back into life.

On the surface, no one suspected anything. The miners started back down the track to the village, and Captain Kewley retired to his bleak house just below the mine workings. He was asleep in bed when faint traces of smoke began to seep out of the top of the shaft.

One hundred and thirty fathoms below, the candle had fallen and ignited the dry wood of the old roof timbers. The fire spread quickly, until with a crash the roof collapsed, and the force of the fall extinguished the flames.

One tragedy had been averted, for a fire would have cost the mine company dearly, but another was just beginning. The roof collapse had put out the fire, but it had also blocked the tunnel, and was preventing the circulation of fresh air. More dangerous still was the charred wood; as it smouldered it gave off a poisonous gas, carbon monoxide, which was invisible, odourless, and deadly.

The next morning, Sunday, there was no sign of either smoke or fire to warn Captain Kewley of the danger below, and so work began normally at 6 a.m. on Monday. The thirty-one underground workers gathered at the top of the shaft to begin their long descent.

It took the first man, Rob Kelly, seventeen minutes to reach the hundred-and-twenty-fathom level. Like the others, he had a small candle fixed to his helmet by a lump of clay—and suddenly, it went out.

"Get to the top, everyone," shouted Kelly. "There's bad air down here." But the candle had given its warning too late. The miners were already breathing the poisonous gas, and had lost all their energy. They couldn't force their legs up even one rung.

Only those near the top were able to escape and give the alarm.

Captain Kewley rushed from his office to begin the daunting task of rescue. Those near the surface were helped up the ladders one by one, but it was a slow business. By mid-afternoon twelve men had been hauled up, some only just alive. The remainder were still in the shaft, and none answered to the rescuers' shouts.

Kewley was determined to get their bodies out. To do this he must be certain that the killer gas had cleared, and there was only one way to find out.

At five o'clock he started back down the shaft. In his hand was a small cage holding five mice. At the ninety-fathom level he stopped, and lowered the cage beneath him on a rope. After waiting two minutes, he hauled it back up; the mice were still alive. He continued down, testing the air every five fathoms. It was a tragic business. The trapped miners were found one by one, all dead. Some were still clinging to the ladders, others lay crumpled on the small platforms that marked the worked-out levels, where they had fallen when their grip gave way.

By mid-afternoon, only one body remained to be found—Rob Kelly's, the man who had led the morning shift—and Captain Kewley had reached the hundred-and-twenty-fathom level.

He peered down into the blackness after the cage. He imagined he could just make out the shape of a man's body on the next platform below. The two minutes were up, and he hauled back the cage. This time there was a difference: one mouse lay motionless in a corner, and at that moment Kewley felt a rush of air flood up into his face. The gas was still there!

He was hauled unconscious up to the surface, the cage still tied to his belt. It was three hours before he came round, to learn that the Mines Inspector had forbidden any further rescue attempt.

He also learnt how close his own escape had been. Of the five mice, four were found to be dead on reaching the surface. The Snaefell shaft, now sealed and flooded, had claimed its last victims.

Two White Mice

To retell the story of the Snaefell mine disaster on film, we went to the ruins of the mine which still stand at the head of the Laxey Valley. Director David Brown set about finding several things to illustrate the action of the story, but sometimes they were unobtainable. The candles for lighting the interior of the mine tunnel were easy to come by, and we borrowed the original piece of charred wood which was all that remained of one of the pit props from a Manxman who lived nearby. His father had actually worked in the mine, and had managed to salvage it after the inquest into the disaster.

The period mouse box was a little more difficult, but after some diligent searching we came up with a nicely-detailed Victorian piece, with delicate wrought iron decorations.

David approached the local pet shop in Douglas, quite confidently, to ask whether he could borrow a couple of white mice for one evening's filming. He was horrified to be told that an expected consignment of white mice had failed to arrive, and all the shelves were bare! The pet shop proprietor tried every mouse owner he knew, but no white mice were forthcoming, and the day for filming was drawing close.

At the eleventh hour, David had a brainwave. He contacted Manx Radio, the local station, and the next morning they appealed, on Blue Peter's behalf, for white mice for filming purposes. But, just to show how difficult life can be, the pet shop's consignment of white mice came in the very same day!

We had arranged for the local vet to bring the mice to the location that evening, so we all met at the disused mine in the dark, set up the cameras, the lights and the props, and then prepared the mice for their starring role. The first few shots were low angles of the mice in the cage being lowered towards the camera, and then hoisted up again. Then we did the same thing with the camera at a higher angle as the cage descended, and then rose up towards the lens.

Anyone coming upon us all in the night, grouped round a shaft, all madly peering into it, with one person holding a long piece of string which disappeared into a black abyss, would certainly have wondered what exactly we were doing!

For that part of the film the mice were, and were seen to be, very lively, but when we repeated the shot for the next part, it was necessary to make one of the mice look as if it had been overcome by fumes from the disaster area in the mine. Hence the presence of the vet.

One mouse was removed from the little cage, and the vet attended to it. It was returned to the cage, and lay in the bottom, looking definitely "unconscious". The vet had warned us that the mouse would only remain "under the influence" for the maximum of one minute, so we set up the shot as fast as we could, lowered the cage out of sight, hauled it up yet again and zoomed in on a close-up of the mouse as the cage neared the camera.

"Cut," shouted David—the camera stopped running, the sound recordist switched off, and, as if by magic, the mouse leapt into action and started scuttling furiously round the cage, squeaking animatedly.

It had given us an Oscar-winning performance!

". . . and exports Kippers!"

Today the Snaefell mountain seems a much more cheerful place than it was in the days of the mining disaster. A branch of the electric tramway takes tourists to the summit, where they can see five countries, England, Scotland, Wales, Ireland, and Man itself. For Snaefell is right at the centre of the island, and the island is right at the centre of the Irish Sea.

On the West Coast of Man, the sea is all important; for the tourists it means quiet beaches and underwater swimming; for the inhabitants it means kippers.

To make kippers, you must first catch your herring, and every evening in the summer the fishing fleet sets sail from Peel harbour. One hundred years ago there were two hundred and thirty fishing boats at Peel; today's fleet is smaller, but the catch is just as big because of improved fishing techniques. In the nineteenth century a man would stand on top of a nearby tower and shout directions to the boats, guiding them to the shoals he could see shimmering in the water, and today's fishermen use a form of radar to find the fish. But some traditions die hard in the Isle of Man: it was always considered unlucky to be the third boat out of harbour, so even now the second and third boats go out lashed together to beat the jinx.

As I watched the fleet sail out into the horizon, I could see why Peel is often called the "Sunset City".

Next morning the boats come back, and the catch is put up to auction.

The auctioneer is surrounded by crates of herrings, knowledgeable buyers, and screaming seagulls as he chants the amount of the bids in a way I found absolutely

Fishing boats in Peel harbour

incomprehensible. Some of the fish are sold directly to foreign buyers, but the majority stay on the island. By nine o'clock the bidding is over, and the fish have been taken up the quay to the kipper houses with the screaming mob of the noisiest, hungriest, largest sea-gulls I have ever seen in anxious attendance.

A kipper is a slit, smoked herring, so the first job is to cut the fish. In the old days there were lines of women with sharp knives, but today the machine has taken over. Next, the slit herrings are soaked in brine for anything up to two hours. The bigger the herring, the longer the soaking. This rule applies to the smoking as well; first the fish are hung on wooden rods, fitted with tenterhooks. These are placed in a tall narrow kiln, until there are thirty thousand kippers all waiting to be smoked. The fuel is hardwood chippings, which are covered with a layer of damp, weathered sawdust, to make sure there's plenty of smoke.

Then it's a case of light the taper and retire immediately! Within seconds the kiln is full of smoke, which is choking and suffocating.

After twelve hours or so the kippers are inspected. If they are still a bit pale the fires are relit, but if they are all a nice toasted brown, out they come, ready for packing.

Kippers are sent all over Britain, but some stay on the island, to be eaten by the trippers, or sent by post, as a "Wish You Were Here" souvenir to friends back home.

And there's never any difficulty in disposing of kippers that don't quite make the grade—for the moment when the waste is thrown out is just what the huge, noisy, impatient seagulls have been waiting for!

People who make their living from the sea are always the first to respect its angry moods. The Irish Sea has always been liable to sudden and violent storms in winter, and in the days of sailing ships wrecks were frequent.

One man who decided to do something about this lived in a house overlooking Douglas Harbour at the beginning of the nineteenth century. His name was Sir William Hillary, and he was to found the world's first volunteer life-saving organisation.

Throughout his life Hillary was an energetic and impulsive man; in 1803 he and his wife were living in Essex when there was a scare that Napoleon might launch an invasion. He immediately raised a legion of troops at his own expense to defend the coastline, and earned himself a knighthood.

But his private Home Guard cost a great deal of money. By 1808 he was penniless, and he retired to the Isle of Man to escape his creditors. By this time his wife felt she had had enough of his escapades, and refused to come with him, but Hillary was undismayed. He decided to remarry, even though she was still alive. His second bride was a Manx girl called Emma Tobin, and he took her across to Gretna Green in Scotland, where the blacksmith was persuaded to perform the ceremony.

It was not until he was fifty years old, ten years after his second marriage, that Hillary found a cause to which he could devote all his energy. Each winter, from his living-room window, he saw ships wrecked in Douglas Bay. There were no long quays in his day, and little shelter during storms. In 1822 half a dozen ships were

The light in Skye changes hundreds of times in the course of the day – with breathtaking results

In the foothills of the Cuillins

Bonnie Prince Charlie kissed Flora MacDonald goodbye
on this spot at the harbour of Portree

With Dame Flora MacLeod of MacLeod and the Fairy Flag
at Dunvegan Castle

"Waulking" the cloth to a song in Gaelic with some
ladies from Skye

Fred and Lesley negotiating a tight corner

I ride round the TT course on Mad Sunday – on a moped!

At 60 m.p.h. the riders take off on Ballaugh Bridge

Queen Victoria thought it was impossible to imagine a prettier spot than her beloved Osborne

Lord Mountbatten told me "Queen Victoria hated smoking, but she once asked my mother for a puff!"

The Governor and Lord Lieutenant of the island the
Earl Mountbatten of Burma, KG, PC, GCB, OM, GCSI, GCIE, GCVO, DSO, FRS

Lord Mountbatten and his grandson Ashley

Queen Victoria's bed with the portrait of her dead
husband hung over the place where he slept

Queen Victoria's bathing machine at Osborne House

wrecked in one month, and many lives lost. With characteristic vigour, Sir William decided to act.

He had little enough money of his own, so he wrote a pamphlet—

"An Appeal
to the
British nation
on the Humanity and Policy
of Forming a National Institution
for the Preservation
of Lives and Property
from Shipwreck."

He still had influential friends in London, and he persuaded them to hold a meeting there in February, 1824. £10,000 was subscribed and the "Shipwreck Institution" was begun. Today we know it as the Royal National Lifeboat Institution, and it still has the three aims that Hillary outlined at that time; it awards medals for bravery, it researches into better ways of saving life, and it builds lifeboats.

Sir William made sure that the Isle of Man was well served, with four lifeboat stations, and there are still four today, the most important in Douglas Harbour, within a stone's throw of his home. Hillary became the first coxswain of the Douglas crew. He had already been awarded one gold medal as Founder of the Institution, but in the next ten years he won three more for bravery. He took part in three hundred and five launchings, and helped to save one hundred and fifteen lives, sometimes in the most perilous conditions.

On 30 November 1830, the cable of the mailboat *St George* snapped in a heavy storm. She was driven out of Douglas Harbour onto the treacherous Conister rocks. The lifeboat put to sea, and managed to pick off the twenty-two man crew by rowing between the rocks and the wreck, but at the cost of breaking the boat's rudder, and smashing six of the ten oars. At one point a huge wave swept Sir William overboard. Amazingly, he had never bothered to learn to swim, but he managed to cling onto the wreckage of the mailboat until he was pulled to safety by oarsman Isaac Vondy.

Sir William immediately offered Vondy a reward, but the Manxman refused: "I don't save lives for gain," he declared.

Hillary came out of all this with six fractured ribs, but it didn't prevent him celebrating his sixtieth birthday a few weeks later. Nor did it stop him writing to the Institution asking for another gold medal for himself, and one for Isaac Vondy!

The Institution gave him no marks for modesty, but they couldn't help marvelling at his bravery and his age, a combination that's still found on the Douglas Lifeboat.

I went out on a practice launch with Coxswain Jack Griffiths and his crew. The weather, I thought, was pretty dreadful; there was a strong wind, with squally showers, the whole time we were on the island.

"It's nothing much today, really, Val," said Jack, as the boat heaved up and down. "When there's a force ten gale, you get waves up to twenty feet high."

I asked him what was the worst wreck he had ever been called out to.

"The worst I ever came to was the *Gretchy*. She was loaded with coal bound for Douglas one terrible day in December about eight years ago. It was five o'clock in the morning, black as pitch, and blowing such a blizzard as we could hardly see to launch the boat. The snow was blowing so hard in our faces, you see. At last we sighted her—run aground off Port Soderick with great terrible waves breaking over her. Ten times we tried to get alongside, but we couldn't get near her because of the weather. I thought it was all up with her, and so did the rest of the boys. We were going to have one more try—when a wonderful strange thing happened!"

"What was that?" I asked.

"The wreck got hit by a giant wave, and it threw her round, broadside on to the weather. That formed a lee—a shelter from the wind—and they were able to launch their rubber lifeboats. The coastguards rescued them from the beach. Every man jack got safely ashore!"

"How many lives have you saved in the twenty years you've been a lifeboatman?" I asked, but I could tell by the look in his eyes that he wasn't going to give me an answer.

"Well—I wouldn't like to say anything about that, like. I mean, you just don't talk about those things."

As far as anyone can make out, Sir William Hillary never retired as a lifeboatman—there were no rules and regulations in his day. He claimed he could still launch a boat single-handed when he was seventy-five.

But his last years were plagued with ill-luck. Once again his careless spending brought him to the verge of bankruptcy; in 1844 he had to sell his fine house and move to lodgings in the town. In 1845 his second wife died, leaving him heartbroken, and he survived her for only two years.

He was buried in a debtor's grave, and it was only the exertions of a few friends that prevented his creditors

Douglas harbour and the tower of refuge

from selling his dead body to the surgeons for medical experiments.

This doesn't mean that Douglas has no memorial to Sir William—he saw to that himself. On Conister Rock, where he had watched so many ships come to grief, he organised the building of a Tower of Refuge. It marked the position of the rock, which is just covered at high tide, and also provide a place of safety where ship-wrecked sailors could take refuge until the storm abated. Salted fish and fresh water were left in the tower, in case the storm should rage for several days.

The tower, which looks like a diminutive Norman castle rising out of the sea, was completed in 1832, and it proved such a good landmark that there has never been a wreck there since. Today it is a favourite place for holiday row-boats to make for, and instead of salted fish, the Tower of Refuge is provisioned with Manx ice cream!

Perhaps Sir William Hillary was a bit of an eccentric, but his Tower of Refuge has withstood the ravages of the sea just as firmly as the Institution he founded one hundred and fifty years ago. He was a true pioneer, and it is perhaps no surprise to learn that one of his distant descendants is Sir Edmund Hillary, the conqueror of Everest.

The R.N.L.I. has no doubt of the debt it owes him; his portrait now appears on all the Institute's medals for bravery, and last year the Isle of Man issued a special set of stamps in his honour.

The Tale of the Manx Cat

The island has been producing its own stamps for two years now, and I thought they were very attractive. They show the horse trams, the Laxey Wheel, the steam railway, the T.T. races, and there's one of the unique Manx breed of sheep, which have four horns. Only a few of these sheep survive. In the same set, the 10p stamp shows another Manx animal that has recently faced extinction—the Manx cat.

It is the tale of the cat with no tail. When the animals were crowding into Noah's Ark, legend says that the very last up the gangway were two Manx cats, which in those far-off days had perfectly normal tails. But like all Manxies they were dawdling—and when the door shut, their tails were chopped off!

A less painful explanation, and a more likely one, is that the Manx cat is a rare mutation of the normal cat.

It wouldn't normally recur, but because the Isle of Man is a small place it is possible that two such mutations might have interbred, and from these two all Manx cats must have descended.

A few years ago it did look as if the Manx cat was disappearing, so the Isle of Man Government set up a special Cattery in Douglas to keep the strain going. It has been a great success, and as well as producing quite a healthy export industry, it is a very popular place for trippers to visit.

I went along too, and I learnt that there are two kinds of Manx cat—some have very tiny tails, and are called "Stumpies", while others have none at all, and are called "rumpies". All of them have long back legs, and a coat that is doubly thick.

Some Manx stamps

I must say I found them rather peculiar at first, but as I played with a group of very appealing kittens I began to realise that these tailless cats have a charm of their own, and I was very glad that the Manx Government is determined they will not become extinct.

So I think it is fair to say that the tale of the Manx cat still has a happy ending!

The Oldest Parliament in the World

The same can't be said for the Manx language, which is, to all intents and purposes, dead. It died because no one ever bothered to write it down, and now it is heard only once a year, at the ancient ceremony of Tynwald, when the titles of the laws passed by the Manx Parliament that year are read out.

The Tynwald claims to be the oldest continuing Parliament in the world. Its day-to-day business is done in Douglas, but every Midsummer Day it assembles at the traditional open-air meeting-place, Tynwald Hill, roughly in the centre of the island.

The hill is scarcely twelve feet high, but it is made up of soil from the seventeen different parishes of Man, and it has stood here for at least five centuries.

The Isle of Man has always been fully independent of Britain; it has the same Queen, but it has different laws, different taxes, and different titles. The Justices are known as Deemsters, the M.P.s are known as Keys, and the highest office is not Prime Minister, but Governor.

As well as *God Save the Queen*, there is a Manx National Anthem, and their flag is not the Union Jack, but the famous three-legged symbol. "Whichever way you throw me, I will stand" is the motto—and for a thousand years the Manx nation has stood proudly on its own three feet.

The Tynwald ceremony is simple but impressive, a reminder that the Manx people have gathered at Tynwald Hill, century after century, since the days of the Vikings, to hear their new laws on Midsummer Day.

T.T. Races

It is a fact too that if it had not been for Tynwald, there would never have been any T.T. races—and nowadays T.T. week is the island's greatest money-spinner.

It all began seventy years ago, when the petrol engine was still very primitive. Motor manufacturers thought a good way to encourage the new industry would be to hold competitive trials, where new machines could be tested to the limit. The snag was that it needed an Act of Parliament to close even the smallest public road for racing, and the British Parliament was much too busy to bother with this.

Not so the Tynwald. The Governor of the day was himself a motor enthusiast, and with his encouragement a special Road Closing Bill was rushed through all the legal processes in less than ten minutes. So in June 1907 the very first race for touring motor-cycles was run.

The first prize was a figure of Mercury, the famous Tourist Trophy. Since then there have been T.T. races every year, except during the two World Wars, and they've proved very popular, not just for those who race, but for those who watch, too.

Anyone with a bike has the chance to try out the

course on the Sunday of T.T. week, when no races are held. The locals call it "Mad Sunday", and I decided I was just mad enough to give it a try, but on the slowest two-wheeler I could find. And I'd been warned to start early, before the big bikes got out.

It was certainly a good way to see the island, and as I plodded on determinedly, I thought that I was going at roughly the speed riders managed on the very first T.T. Their bikes had no gears, and even the man who won the race had to get off and push up the steepest hill on the course.

Since then speeds have increased dramatically, to fifty miles an hour in 1920, ninety in 1950, and anything up to a hundred and twenty today, and hills are no longer any real problem.

The challenge of the T.T. today is to ride as fast as possible within the limitations of the course. It's not like racing on a specially built circuit; the roads are sometimes narrow, the surface often rough, and the route is thirty-seven and three-quarter miles long. To win the T.T. you really have got to know every single bend by heart—and there are over a hundred of them.

Ballaugh Bridge is one of the trickiest; it is a bend with a hump-backed bridge, which means some bikes become airborne for a few yards—going at four times the speed I managed!

The most attractive part of the course is beyond Ramsey, the seaside resort in the north of the island. It follows the old mountain road high up onto the slopes of Snaefell. It is also the most popular stretch with the bike enthusiasts, who began to catch up with me as the Sunday morning wore on. This is the fastest part of the circuit; the bends are gentle and there are no hedges or buildings to obscure the riders' view ahead —a far cry from the early days, when the road was little more than a cart-track, and one of the racers' biggest worries was dodging sheep!

Once past Snaefell the road makes a fast descent back into Douglas, and I decided to play safe, and let the big bikes go first.

The T.T. races have various classifications—Senior for 500cc, Junior for 300cc, and so on. The most popular with the spectators is the sidecar T.T., so on the Sunday evening I went along to see the competitors getting their bikes ready. Amongst them I found a husband and wife team, Fred and Lesley Lewin.

I expected the sidecar to look like ordinary sidecars I'd seen on the roads, but I was in for a shock. A racing sidecar is nothing more than a narrow platform on which the passenger lies flat on her tummy.

Lesley, a pretty, dark, forthright girl showed me what happens when she and Fred take bends when every second counts.

"On a right-hand bend I leave the sidecar and climb up behind Fred."

"And on a left-hand bend?"

"On a left-hand bend I climb back over the sidecar, grab hold of that hand grip, and lean out as far as I can."

"But don't you fall off?—I mean, your bottom's almost touching the ground."

"It does touch the ground," said Fred proudly.

"It's quite easy really," said Lesley, "because you're balancing against gravity. If you're in the right position it's no effort at all."

It was Fred and Lesley's fifth T.T. and I asked

Lesley how she started sidecar racing.

"It was nine years ago when I was still at school. Fred was trying out a bike at Brand's Hatch, and I went along just to watch. Fred said: 'Why don't you have a try, just sitting on the sidecar—you don't have to move—just sit there!' I said: 'You must be joking!'— you know—'You'll never get me on one of them!'"

"Anyway, ten laps later, she'd got the bug!" Fred took up the story.

Lesley grinned back at him admiringly. "And I've been doing it ever since!"

The next morning it was business as usual on the T.T. course. The Tynwald's Road Closing Order stipulated 10.40 a.m. as the time when the course should be cleared. The job is organised by the island's Chief Constable, from the central control box overlooking the grandstand.

At the precise time the signal is given, and all round the island an army of temporary wardens and policemen spring into action. Barriers are swung across every road leading onto the course. In five minutes, as if by magic, a meandering country road is transformed into the most famous and perhaps the most dangerous motor cycling race course in the world.

Racing cyclists from all over Europe were revving up their engines on the starting grid. The Germans were hotly fancied again this year, particularly Siegfried Schauzu and Wolfgang Kalauch.

I waved good luck to Fred and Lesley, and watched the tall sinister figures of Siegfried and Wolfgang closing down the visors on their helmets.

Contrasting with the international set was a pack of cub scouts in uniform standing by to chalk up the course timings on the grandstand boards.

It is a staggered start, because a mass take-off of seventy or so bikes would result in chaos.

The first lap went very well for Fred and Lesley. They were among the leaders, and with two laps to go, it was not a bad position. Wolfgang and Siegfried, however, were lying first, with every intention of staying there.

It was in the third lap that disaster struck. This is Lesley's account of it: "We were coming down the main Sulby straight, not quite so fast as the first two laps, which was lucky. I remember seeing three bikes just in front, and I knew there were two not far behind, and I thought 'I hope there's not too many of us when we get to the bottom, because it's a very tight corner, and they've put down new tarmac there!'

"Fred slowed right down as we came to the bridge, and I remember thinking, 'Well, he's making sure we all get through.' Then suddenly we started going sideways across the road. Fred was fighting all the way round—we were nearly there—when the handgrip just clipped the wall. The next thing I knew, I was flying through the air.

"I think if the man from the St John's Ambulance hadn't been so good, I'd have got back up and finished the race. But this heavy doctor was sitting in the middle of my chest, saying, 'Lie perfectly still!' and after a few minutes I decided he had the better idea!"

"What actually went wrong?" I asked her.

"One of the marshals said we were touched by another bike—I don't know. If we were, it certainly wasn't intentional. Perhaps it was oil, or that new tarmac—or a combination of all three. Whatever it was—it was the end for this year."

"And what about next year?"

"Oh, we'll be going back. I was robbed—make no mistake about it!"

It was Siegfried and Wolfgang who took the chequered flag, and the trophy, and the glory. The West German flag broke over the rostrum, and the band struck up the West German national anthem.

For Siegfried and Wolfgang, another race is over—but that isn't the end of the T.T. spectacle. Immediately the marshals start the operation of reopening the roads. A "Roads Open" car sets off round the course as soon as the last bike has started the last lap. Once it has passed by, the road behind is officially open to traffic, and the spectators pour onto the track.

The Chief Constable told me that he found this the most frightening part of the T.T., as the would-be racers emulate their heroes and try to be first back to Douglas. But the road-opening certainly works; within an hour the island was amazingly back to normal, until the next T.T.

Time Enough

There is one Manx saying which *has* survived to the present day—"Oh, traie di lhooa." It means: "There's always time enough"—but I don't agree.

My Isle of Man Assignment was all too short, and there is a great deal on the island I had no time to see.

Perhaps Manx sayings are only intended for the Manx people, and for the lucky ones who live on their attractive island, I can well imagine there will always be "time enough".

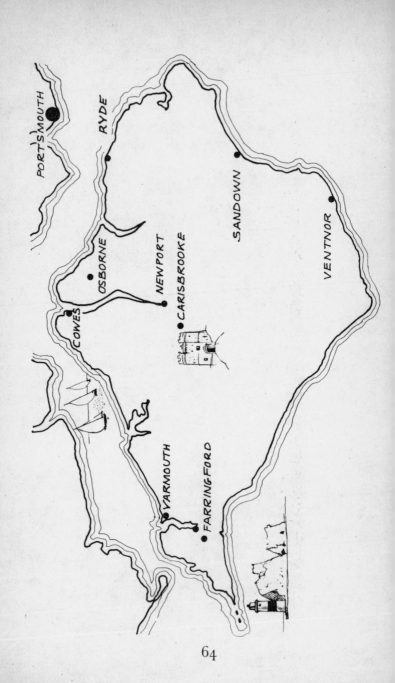

ISLE OF WIGHT

Two Thousand Years of Holidays

The Isle of Wight has been a holiday island for hundreds of years, and it's the oldest holiday resort in the whole of the British Isles.

The Romans visited it nearly two thousand years ago—they called it Vectis. On the island's peaceful sunny slopes they built elegant villas, open to the sun and the cool winds from the sea. Here, too, they planted vineyards; Vectis wine was known for its fragrance, and indeed wine is still produced every year from vines grown on the very same slopes.

Along the shores and tiny inland creeks, the Romans dredged for oysters, which they thought were a great delicacy, and today, after two thousand years, the Isle of Wight still has a flourishing oyster trade.

The Romans left little behind them, but in their footsteps came thousands of people to explore the delights of the island, from ordinary holiday makers to Queen Victoria herself. She came first as a Princess, when she was still a little girl; she immediately fell in love with the Isle of Wight, and decided she would always come back.

Now thousands of holidaymakers arrive every year, by the ferries. Many of them, like me, choose the fast exciting Hovercraft.

Hovercraft are a familiar sight in the waters round Cowes where they land, because the factory that makes them is actually on the island. The journey from Southampton took us only twenty minutes, and we landed on time after our flight—for although the craft just skims the surface of the waves, the journey is actually called a flight!

The Smugglers, the Maze, and the Monsters

Some of the most unusual visitors ever to fly in to the Isle of Wight arrived by helicopter in 1972—they were enormous life-sized dinosaurs. They were not strangers to me, because I, and millions of Blue Peter viewers, watched as John Noakes helped with this extraordinary airlift, and guided the monsters to their permanent home.

They were installed as part of a famous park on the island, called Blackgang Chine. Chine means a valley, and the Blackgang part came from a notorious gang of smugglers who worked along the coast. The valley is a deep cleft between the cliffs, with steep slopes and tall trees, and it was made into a place of entertainment and opened to the public in 1843.

The monsters certainly look well settled in now, surrounded by greenery, and seem to peer through the trees—they could have been established for thousands of years instead of just three. But they must be rather surprised at some of their neighbours, because in the island's largest entertainment park there is something for everyone.

The gnomes' garden always has crowds of visitors, and so does the model of a smuggler's cave, and the model village.

One of the favourite attractions is the maze, where people come just to show how easily they can master it. Like me, they enter boldly enough, and make their way between the six-foot-high thick green hedges. I knew what to do—there's a special way of getting out of a maze—you just keep turning right all the time, and you get out in no time at all, I was told. So I tried.

After ten minutes, I was back at the beginning, but that wasn't good enough—I wanted to come out by the real exit, so I plunged in again. After another quarter of an hour, I would have settled gladly for the entrance —every turn brought me up to a tall six-foot green wall. I could hear people the other side—I knew there must be a way out—but how could I find it? I began to feel hungry, and I wondered if the maze was checked when Blackgang Chine closed for the night. Then I remembered that that day was the special Late Night Opening!

Isle of Wight hovercraft

Suddenly, I was there, outside and in the sunshine again. Very relieved, I made my way to the Blackgang Souvenir Bazaar.

"What's the maze like, Val?" the Blue Peter crew asked me.

"Oh, it's easy," I replied. "You really ought to try it yourself."

Twenty-eight Different Coloured Sands

You can buy all kinds of souvenirs in the shop at Blackgang Chine, from a model of the Needles lighthouse to a small replica of the dinosaurs. The best sellers, though, were something I had not seen before—different shapes of thin glass, which looked as if they had been painted with waving multi-coloured stripes. When I looked closely I realised the stripes weren't painted on—the glasses were hollow, like bottles, and they were filled up with layers of different coloured sand. They were very attractive, with a dozen shades arranged very prettily in swirling patterns.

Sand jars like these have been sold on the Isle of Wight since Victorian times, and all the sand inside them comes from one particular part of the coast—Alum Bay. At that point, the cliffs are made up of sand which has formed itself into patterns and layers of twenty-eight different colours. It's still a popular place, but it has always been difficult to get down the steep crumbling cliffs, so today there is a route the Victorians certainly didn't use—a chair-lift!

I felt very precarious and open to the elements as my metal chair swung high over the tree tops and then dropped sharply down, but it is perfectly safe. There was a path far below my feet which has been in use for many years, for people who didn't fancy travelling my way.

In former times, people walked down the steep path and collected their own sand samples from the cliff. But over the years the cliffs started to slip away, so today visitors are asked not to dig for themselves any more, as it wastes a lot of sand and now it's quite a dangerous thing to do.

So today there are stalls where you can buy the sand, and the glass containers to put it in. I bought my little bottle, but as I looked along the trays of sand, I didn't see how I'd fit them all in. There was gold, brown, and chalky white, grey, brick-coloured—I'd never imagined so many kinds! The stallholder told me the art is to take just a bit of sand with a scoop like a mustard spoon, then another, then press them down hard with a little stick, which makes the ripple effect.

After a few minutes, the stallholder pressed a cork in for me, and I emerged with the finished article—I didn't think it would win any prizes or end up at the National Gallery, but I had done it all myself, and I knew I would take it proudly back home with me, like so many other visitors to the Isle of Wight.

But filling bottles with the sand isn't the only thing you can do—you can actually paint pictures with the sand for colours. The Victorians were very fond of doing it, and they spent ages sprinkling the different colours on to glue, to get really natural-looking effects.

They liked best to make pictures of favourite views and buildings on the Isle of Wight, particularly the two most famous, Osborne House and Carisbrooke Castle.

The Man who Tweaked Queen Victoria's Nose

Carisbrooke, the ancient Castle built in 1100, has long been a part of the island's history, and the traditional seat of the Governor of the Isle of Wight. Until recently, the Governor of the Island has been Earl Mountbatten of Burma, the Queen's cousin. Then the government decided to make the Isle of Wight a County in its own right, so it wouldn't need a Governor any more, but a Lord Lieutenant. The Island was overjoyed to learn that their first Lord Lieutenant would be—Earl Mountbatten of Burma!—so a special ceremony was arranged at Carisbrooke Castle, for everyone to say how pleased they were.

The fanfare of trumpets rang out, and the standard of the Mountbatten family broke on the flagstaff high above the Keep. Lord Mountbatten, now seventy-three years old, stooping slightly, but still strikingly handsome in his uniform of Admiral of the Fleet, stepped out of his limousine and began to inspect the Guard of Honour mounted to receive the Governor and Lord Lieutenant of the Isle of Wight.

Later on, I asked him if there were any other duties involved in the governorship, apart from attending official functions.

"Not really," he smiled. "Most of my powers have been whittled away. When my aunt, Princess Henry Battenberg, was Governor, she was also Coroner of the Isle of Wight, whereas I'm not allowed to go near a corpse. I've even got instructions in my patent not to meddle with the ferry!"

Lord Mountbatten's family have been connected with the island since Queen Victoria's time. After the ceremony at Carisbrooke he took his grandson, Ashley

The gateway to Carisbrooke Castle

71

Hicks, aged eleven, to Osborne, to show him round the house which his great-grandmother, Queen Victoria, and his great-grandfather, Prince Albert, had built for their summer retreat.

They paused by the famous Winterhalter picture of the Royal Family, Lord Mountbatten's hands resting on Ashley's shoulders as they looked up at the enormous portrait.

"There you can see my great-grandmother, Queen Victoria—that's your great-great-great-grandmother. And with her is your great-great-great-grandfather, the Prince Consort."

When I talked to Lord Mountbatten afterwards, I asked him if he had ever met Queen Victoria.

"Well, I don't know what you call 'meeting her'. If you 'meet' someone at your christening, then I did, it's true. I'm told she held me on that occasion, and the Lady-in-waiting who handed me over to Queen Victoria says I tweaked her nose, and I think I pulled her spectacles off—so I must have known her fairly well!"

Queen Victoria became a legend in her own lifetime, and hundreds of stories have been written about her. I asked Lord Mountbatten if there were any particular family stories that we might not have heard.

"The one I like best is a story I heard from my mother.

"As you know, Queen Victoria was absolutely bitterly opposed to smoking. No one—not even her family—was allowed to smoke in any of her palaces. The Prince of Wales, King Edward VII used to go through every sort of contortion to try and find a place where his mother wouldn't smell his cigar smoke. The Prime Minister used to come and lie with his head in the fireplace, hoping that the old lady wouldn't smell it. They all had to pretend they weren't smoking.

"But not my mother. She never hid anything. She just smoked. She didn't actually smoke in the presence of the Queen and puff the smoke in her face, but as soon as the Queen found out, she said, 'Victoria, is it true you smoke?' She said, 'Yes, of course!'

"One day, they were out walking together, and there were a lot of midges about. The Queen said 'There are a lot of midges here—just light up a cigarette and it will drive them away,' so my mother lit up a cigarette.

"Queen Victoria was fascinated, and said: 'I think I'd like to try one. Will you light one for me?'

"So my mother lit a cigarette for the old Queen, who puffed away. Then she said: 'It's absolutely horrible!' —and threw it away!'"

I asked Lord Mountbatten what he thought Queen Victoria would think of the Isle of Wight today.

"Well, of course it's a very difficult thing to put oneself in the mind of *the* Victoria—but, funnily enough, I think the Isle of Wight, and perhaps Balmoral, are the two places that have changed least. I think she'd still be at home here—much more than she would be at Buckingham Palace! She'd be absolutely lost in London, and pretty lost in Windsor, but not in the Isle of Wight.

"The Isle of Wight has remained agreeably old-fashioned. It's retained a lot of its Victorian charm, even though it's been brought up to date for comfort— and I don't think Queen Victoria would have objected to that!"

Queen Victoria, the great-grandmother of Lord Mountbatten, ruled her Empire and lived in royal palaces in great state, but she was also a wife and mother. She and Prince Albert, her husband, wanted a real home for their growing family—"a place of one's own, quiet and retired"—the Queen declared. She remembered her happy holidays on the Isle of Wight, and inquiries were put in hand. Albert wrote careful letters asking about the sea view, the water supply, and the public footpaths that might be fatal to privacy. All the answers were satisfactory, so the Royal Family arrived. Victoria was enchanted, and said so.

"The Queen thinks it is impossible to imagine a prettier spot, woods and valleys which would be beautiful anywhere, but all this near the sea, is quite perfection! We have a charming beach quite to ourselves. The sea is so blue and calm, the Prince says it is like Naples. And then, we can walk anywhere by ourselves, without fear of being followed and mobbed, which is delightful."

The new house—Her Majesty's Marine Residence at Osborne—was designed by Prince Albert, with the professional help of architect Thomas Cubitt. Filled with ideas of Naples, he tried to achieve an Italian summer palace. Not everyone liked it. One courtier complained: "It is very ugly, and the whole concern wretched. They will spend first and last a great deal of money there, but it is her own money and not the nation's."

That was the great advantage—it was the Queen's *own* home, not a royal palace, hemmed in with restrictions. "Here we are free from all the government departments which really are the plague of one's life," she exclaimed thankfully.

From the first moment that Victoria walked through the rooms at Osborne, and looked out into the gardens, bright with flowering shrubs, she loved it all. "It is my dearest Albert's own creation, own work, own building and laying out!"

On 16 September 1846 they dined in the new dining-room for the first time. The members of the Royal Household drank their health, and Albert replied: "We have a German hymn for occasions like this. It says 'May God bless this house, and bless our going out and our coming in'."

From that first evening, life at Osborne took on its regular pattern. After dinner, the Queen sat in the drawing-room with her ladies. Close at hand, Albert would play billiards on the table he had designed himself. The gentlemen of the court could sit down, for a few grateful moments, on a bench that ran along the wall, because they were round the corner, and, technically, not in the Queen's presence.

The downstairs rooms were large and sumptuous, and provided a fitting setting for a Queen and her household, even on holiday, but once upstairs, we seem to enter a different world—the private apartments. "Secret and Confidential" might be written on the door; so few strangers ever entered them, they still breathe an air of privacy.

In the long summer evenings, the Queen and her husband would stand together on the balcony listening to the nightingales singing in the woods by the sea.

Albert had designed the rooms, and they were very

practical: his bath was of the latest design, and the Queen's bath was a great innovation.

Cosy chintz, family photographs and pictures of favourite pets made the rooms homely and comfortable, very much like the homes of many of their subjects. Albert's walking sticks stood ready for his long walks round the estate.

In the Queen's bedroom, her dressing-table had a leaf which pulled out for writing on. Here, every night of her life, she wrote her journal about the events of the day. "How happy we are here!" she wrote, "and never do I enjoy myself more, or more peacefully, than when I can be so much with my beloved Albert, and follow him everywhere."

The Queen could never escape long from state business, even in her holiday home. She used to work for several hours each day at her desk in the private sitting-room. At a desk exactly like hers, but higher—for the Queen was a very tiny lady—sat Albert, always close by, ready to help, drafting letters and notes, and handing them to her, to read and sign.

"I am happy," said the Queen, "in the solid pleasures of a peaceful, quiet, yet merry life, with my inestimable husband and friend. No sovereign was more loved than I am—from our happy domestic home, which gives such a good example."

The royal nurseries were on the floor above, and reminders of family life were everywhere—strange white marble carvings of the limbs of the royal children—photographs of them in plays they acted for their parents—a programme of a concert they gave on their mother's birthday; just like any parents, keeping programmes and photographs of school plays.

There were nine children, and the summer holidays in Osborne, from the middle of July to the end of August, were the magic time of the year. The children had their own secret places, along the little paths lined with trees and flowers, where few grown-ups ever followed them. And there was their own house—a little chalet called the Swiss Cottage. It was ordered by Prince Albert for his children, and really did come from Switzerland, in sections, and was put up in the grounds, for their very own use.

In the tiny cottage, the royal princesses could make cakes, and invite their parents to tea. The royal princes could try their hand at collecting rocks, or spiders, or birds' eggs, and the very little ones could play shop, in a model grocer's shop which, naturally, carried a Royal Warrant to supply the Queen!

Prince Arthur, the Queen's seventh child, was named after the aged hero, the Duke of Wellington, who was his godfather. He was always fascinated by the army; at Osborne he had his own stronghold, Fort Albert, with barracks and fortifications and cannon, to play soldiers on a grand scale. Much later, little Arthur was to become Field Marshal, the Duke of Connaught.

If the Queen felt inclined to sample their own charming beach, she had her own bathing machine, though she was rather dubious at first. "Drove down to the beach with my maids and went into the bathing machine, where I undressed and bathed in the sea for the first time in my life. I thought it delightful, till I put my head under the water, when I thought I should be stifled."

Near the Swiss Cottage stands a thatched shed that still holds a collection of gardening implements the

The Swiss Cottage in the gardens at Osborne

royal children used in their own gardens. They are marked with their initials, for the Prince of Wales, the Princess Royal, Princess Alice, and so on—spades, and brooms, and little wheelbarrows. Perhaps, years later when they grew up, and became King Edward VII, the Empress of Germany, the Grand Duchess of Hesse, they looked back on those golden days.

"We are more and more delighted with this lovely spot," the Queen said, again and again. "It is to us a perfect little Paradise." It was their summer Paradise for fifteen years. Then everything changed.

Prince Albert became ill and died; his wife was at his bedside. "Oh, my dear darling!" she cried in despair.

Victoria, at forty-two, was now a lonely and grief-stricken widow. Desperately she tried to cling to the past. Nothing was to change—everything was to be as Albert left it. The pocket for Albert's watch stayed in its usual place at the head of the bed, and above his pillow hung a picture of him as he lay dead. Beside the bed stood the Queen's favourite picture of him, as a knight in shining armour.

"I only live through him, the Heavenly Angel. My only wish is to join him soon. I try to comfort myself by knowing that he is always near me, although invisible."

Slowly she took up life again. Once more she worked at her desk in the sitting-room. As her children married and grandchildren were born, Osborne once more became the scene of family parties and picnics. The family grew, and Victoria was surrounded by children, grandchildren and great-grandchildren, married into every royal family in Europe.

Sixty years after she had come to the throne, she was still Queen and Empress ruling a vast Empire. She still loved Osborne, and to the end she enjoyed a quiet drive through the grounds that Albert had planned.

At last she died, at Osborne, at the age of eighty-one, as the new century was beginning. She was surrounded by her family, supported by the son who was to become Edward VII and the grandson who was the Emperor of Germany, the Kaiser.

In the floor of the dining-room, where Albert had replied to the toast that first evening at Osborne, a tablet has been placed, to mark the spot where the Queen's coffin rested. She lay in state for ten days, guarded by four grenadiers, the crown on her coffin. Then for the last time she left Osborne.

It was a solemn, majestic occasion, in the depths of winter, very different from the days of the fifteen summers she had passed there as a young wife and mother. Her funeral procession filed across the court-yard, past the main entrance of the house where she had once been so happy.

It carried her first to London, then to Windsor, to lie beside Albert, who had died forty years before.

Star Turn

After all the splendours of Lord Mountbatten's visit to Carisbrooke Castle, I went back again next day, less ceremoniously, because there was something else there I wanted to see very much.

In a paddock in the castle grounds there is a group of very well-fed and well-cared-for donkeys. All the tourists go to see them, but they are not there just to provide a picturesque scene—they are real working donkeys.

For hundreds of years, the only water supply at Carisbrooke was from a well, fed by an underground stream inside a Well House, and a most ingenious way was devised for drawing up the water.

I went into the Well House, and waited with a group of visitors in the narrow space by the well head, for this to be demonstrated. Over the well itself was a huge wooden wheel, with a solid rim about two feet wide. A rope dangled down into the darkness below.

At length there was a clip-clop of approaching hooves, and Alf Bigwood came into the Well House, leading a very self-possessed little donkey. Alf took up his position beside the wheel, and without a word from him, the donkey took up *her* position—inside the wheel.

Slowly and steadily the donkey started walking. The movement set the wheel turning, and the rope dropped further and further down into the blackness.

All the time, Alf Bigwood told us some facts and figures about this elaborate performance. The rope is a hundred and eighty feet long, and there is a bucket at the end of it. As the bucket reaches the water, it fills, and the mechanism of the wheel is so finely balanced that the additional weight is enough to start bringing the bucket up again. The donkeys, he told us, each took six months to train. They worked for an hour, then had two hours break.

By this time the bucket had come to the surface. Alf took a jugful of the water, and poured it back into the well. There was a very, very, long pause, before we heard the splash as it hit the surface of the water far below. We gasped in amazement.

The show was over. We clapped and murmured approval. The donkey, again without a word of

81

command, had stepped quietly outside the wheel, and stood waiting.

The tourists shuffled out through the exit door. Another group began to come in through the entrance, for the donkey at the Well House is one of the most popular sights on the island.

Fully aware of it, the donkey stood by, very composed, ready for the next performance, when all eyes would be upon her, as once more she presented her star turn.

The Bard of Farringford

Over on the south-west corner of the island, in the peaceful setting of the downs, stands an elegant country house I went to visit. Like Osborne, it was a place of refuge for an eminent Victorian–Alfred, Lord Tennyson, the Poet Laureate.

Tennyson was acclaimed and admired everywhere. The Prince Consort respected him; everyone bought his poems and quoted them. He was more than popular, he was a national institution.

Out of his success, he bought his house, Farringford. It is a hotel now, but I could easily see how the house and garden, set in the quiet countryside, appealed to the poet longing for beauty and peace. Inside the house, too, the calm atmosphere remains—though some changes have had to be made for the hotel guests. I wondered what the original owner would have thought of a notice which read: *Tennyson's Study— Colour Television Room*! But even when it was the poet's private house, there were a great many guests, for the Tennysons were hospitable people, and their friends

82

followed them to visit them in their hide-away.

After dinner they gathered in the drawing-room, to hear their host read his own verses aloud to them. As he did so, he seemed transformed, reading with the authority of a prophet. They listened spellbound to the lines that had made him the most famous poet of his day:

> *Half a league, half a league,*
> *Half a league onward,*
> *Into the Valley of Death*
> *Rode the Six Hundred.*

Then he would change again, and become once more his gruff, kindly, short-sighted self. Once, as he held up his candle to go to bed, his beard caught fire. A friend hurried up to put it out.

"Oh, never mind!" exclaimed Tennyson. "It depends upon chance burnings!"

Queen Victoria greatly admired the poet, and used to invite him to Osborne. He sent her special poems and wrote letters to her, calling her "Dear and Honoured Lady."

Like all public figures, he was followed by abusive letters, which made him miserable. One letter from a writer completely unknown to him railed: "Sir— Once I worshipped you—now I loathe you, you beast!" But even worse were the flocks of admirers, fans, who crossed the ferry, jogged over the bad island roads, and thronged round the garden to catch a glimpse of their idol. "Great men are like pigs, ripped open by the public" he declared frantically.

Today it seems strange that a *poet* should be mobbed and acclaimed in a way we associate with pop singers, but certainly Tennyson was as eager as Queen Victoria to find a secret place of his own on the island, because

Farringford, the home of Lord Tennyson

visitors continued to pester him. One day he was having lunch with his family when he looked up and saw a nose flattened against the window, and heard a voice shouting gleefully: "You can see him well from here!"

He became so nervous of the unwelcome crowds that once, on a walk, he fled in alarm from a flock of sheep, because he thought they were admirers advancing towards him.

He would seek sanctuary at the top of the house, in his own study, with his pipes, his books, his desk and his view. Here the Bard of Farringford, as the eager throng called him, wrote the tremendous poems that made him even more popular—*Maud*, *The Revenge*, and the series of legends of King Arthur, *Idylls of the King*.

Yet even here he was not entirely secure. Sometimes the unwanted guests actually got into the house. He would hear them in the corridor, but he had his escape route ready. He seized the great cloak and the wide hat he always wore, and hurried down a secret staircase, desperately rushing to the fresh air. He would hasten across the lawn towards a secret way out of the garden, and from there he could make his way up on to the high downs that he loved best.

Today a great cross stands there, looking out to sea, a monument his friends raised after his death, but his best memorial is High Down itself, which today is called Tennyson Down.

Here at last he felt free and alone, able to stride along, tossed by the wind, breathing the sharp air, and turning over in his mind the lines of the great poems inspired by his beautiful countryside:

> *"Calm and deep peace on this high wold*
> *And on these dews that drench the furze.*
> *Calm and still light on yon great plain,*
> *That sweeps with all its autumn bowers*
> *And crowded farms and lessening towers*
> *To mingle with the bounding main:*
> *Calm on the seas and silver sleep*
> *And waves that sway themselves in rest."*

Marooned on a Lighthouse

The sea battering the cliffs near Tennyson Down is often far from calm. It can be treacherous, and standing guard at the most westerly point of the island is one of the most famous lighthouses in the world.

It is called the Needles, and you can see why after one glance at the jagged rocks which stretch in a line back to the coast.

The first Needles Lighthouse was built in 1785, and was lit according to a Trinity House Charter which declared that lights should be "kept burning in the night season, whereby seafaring men and mariners might take notice of and avoid dangers, and ships and other vessels of war might safely cruise during the night season in the English Channel."

The lighthouse that stands off the Isle of Wight today was built in 1859, and I was very pleased when the Principal Keeper, Mr Brian Harris, invited me to look round. I thought it would be exciting, but I had no idea how exciting it would actually turn out to be.

The tides off the Needles are very tricky, and to get there on the best day for filming meant an early start for the whole Blue Peter crew. It was at three o'clock in the morning that seven alarm clocks rang, and seven people dragged themselves out of bed, groping for the light switches. We piled on warm, waterproof clothes, and drove to Totland Pier.

I stood on the end of the pier, in the pitch dark, with Director Sarah Hellings, Jane her assistant, and the crew, all straining our ears and eyes for Tony Isaacs who was bringing his boat for us—in the dark at half-past three in the morning it seemed rather improbable.

At last we heard the faint puttering of a boat's engine, and before long, all of us, and all our gear, were safe at the lighthouse, after a smooth twenty-minute crossing.

Brian Harris, the keeper, handed us ashore, and

soon we were making plans for breakfast. There are usually three men on duty at a lighthouse, so an extra seven visitors strained their resources!

Brian showed us round, and we started filming—we saw how the light worked, and how the men lived and worked on their tour of duty, and we saw how Beamish, the tame seagull, landed on the windowsill to be fed.

Time seemed to fly by. It was hours later that we went on to the balcony, to see the foghorns that are switched on when visibility is too poor for the flashing red and green and white lights to be clear. Then, for the first time, we noticed how rough the sea had become.

Tony and his boat were meant to be coming for us at the next high tide, which would be about two in the afternoon, but there was no sign of him, and although the sun was shining through gaps in the clouds, the sea was getting fresher, and spray was being hurtled right over the landing stage. We packed our gear, piled it on the jetty, and waited until half-past three, when we saw a small bobbing speck—the boat, making its way towards us. Aboard her were Tony and his mate, dressed from head to foot in shiny yellow oilskins, three relief lighthouse keepers who were going to do the change-over that day, their gear, and their supplies of food for a month.

In the heavy seas, it seemed impossible for the boat to moor alongside the steps, but there were three people and their gear to disembark, and ten people plus all their gear, to go aboard. It was quite a problem.

A human chain was organised down to the bottom step—the unfortunate person at the end got completely drenched when there was a bigger than usual wave—while Tony manoeuvred the boat as close in as possible,

The Needles

keeping a careful eye on the racing water, to make sure he wasn't driven on the rocks.

The three relief lighthouse keepers scrambled off the heaving boat, with all the skill gained through years of service with Trinity House, and then the stuff in the boat was thrown up to the chain of people gathering on the jetty. After twenty minutes, we started the process in reverse, and soon we had the satisfaction of seeing all our filming equipment and lighting gear in the boat.

Keeper Brian Harris was in the boat too, his shirt sleeves rolled up in a very business-like way, his life-jacket firmly strapped on.

"Start getting the personnel aboard now," he ordered.

That meant us!

"Val first," everyone said politely, so I stood on the bottom step, with Doug, another keeper, firmly grasping my elbow, while Tony once more worked his boat towards the lighthouse.

"Whatever you do," shouted Brian, "don't go until I say so, and don't jump, *step* on to the side of the boat, and I'll look after you from there."

The boat drew alongside—I stretched out my arms to Brian—he reached for me—a large wave broke— the boat surged back from the steps, and our hands were wrenched apart.

This happened five times. Each time the boat had to stand well off and negotiate its approach all over again.

My trousers were sopping wet by now, and so were Sarah's—she was standing on the step above me, waiting for her turn. The spray seemed to be getting higher, and the wind was rougher.

The boat drew near yet again. Brian grinned at me.

"I'll get you this time, Val," he called.

We both reached out our hands—they gripped.

"Now!" Brian yelled, over the wind. I drew a deep breath, and stepped out, on to the side of the boat—and in, helped by Brian. The crew cheered faintly.

Now it was Sarah's turn; and while I huddled up in the bottom of the boat, not to get in the way, we approached once more. At the fourth attempt she was half-pulled into the boat, as it rose on a wave to meet her.

Jane tried next. She stood bravely ready, but this time Brian cupped his hands round his mouth, and shouted, "We can't make it. It's getting too rough. See you at five tomorrow morning."

The boat circled, and sped off to Totland Pier once more. Sarah and I waved wildly with one hand and clung to the boat with the other, and the forlorn group at the foot of the lighthouse grew smaller and smaller. There they were, marooned on a lighthouse, and the wind might not die down for days.

When—eventually—I saw Jane, once more, I asked what the adventure had been like.

"We weren't really marooned," she said, "that sounds too dramatic."

"Was there anything to eat?"

"Oh, yes, we had bangers and mash for supper—the lighthouse men kindly opened their stores, and Mick, the camera assistant and I peeled the potatoes. Then we all watched *Top of the Pops* on the lighthouse television."

"Was there anywhere to sleep?"

"Well, beds were in short supply, but I had a little box at the top of a ladder, with a nice thick curtain to draw across. I thought at first I'd never get to sleep, with the light flashing all the time, but I'd forgotten that we got up at three in the morning. It was the best night's sleep I've ever had."

"When did you get off in the end?"

"When Brian had said—five the next morning. It was grey and chilly, but the sea was much calmer, so when the boat came we all got on first time; and began heading for Totland Pier. I expect the lighthouse keepers breathed a sigh of relief!"

"But really," I insisted, "you could have been there for days, or wrecked getting back, or anything. What did you think when you got back on dry land?"

"We all wondered where on the Isle of Wight you can get a slap-up breakfast at five-thirty in the morning!"

Cowes Week

For one week in the year this little off-shore island becomes the most fashionable place in Europe, and the greatest marine sporting centre in the world.

The Royal Yacht *Britannia* steams up the Solent every August with the Royal Family aboard, and yachts and yachtsmen, from fully-crewed ocean-going racers to tiny single-handed dinghies, transform the harbour into a glittering international scene, for Cowes Week. "Cowes Roads" is a forest of masts, and the little sleepy town is thronged with people in crew-neck sweaters and rubber-soled shoes by day, who emerge in dinner suits and long evening dresses when the sun goes down over the yardarm. Every day is a racing day, and every night is party night, during Cowes Week.

They say that if you walk along the jetty in Cowes Week you are sure to meet someone you know. I felt fairly sceptical about this, as I didn't think *I* knew anybody in the sailing world, but I hadn't walked more than a hundred yards when I heard someone shout, "Hello, Val!" Within minutes I was drinking tea aboard the *Priority* with Robin Walters, who was a friend I hadn't seen for ages.

"I didn't know you were a sailor," I remarked.

"I didn't know you were, either," he replied, eyeing my jeans and oilskin jacket. I didn't have time to explain that I was only being a sailor for the day.

I had been invited to join Christopher Sharples the skipper of the *Alaunt of Corfe* for a race of twenty-five miles along the coast, and back. The *Alaunt* is a fifty-three-foot Class One Ocean Racer, which carries a crew of ten. The race was due to start at 10.30, from a point just off the Royal Yacht Squadron Quay. The Royal Yacht Squadron is a member of the joint committee which controls all the races in Cowes Week. The starting point is called the "line"; it is not literally a line, of course, but an imaginary line that stretches from Squadron Quay to a buoy across the harbour. You have to get your boat as close to the line as possible when the starting gun is fired. If you cross the line before the gun, you would be disqualified, but get too far behind and you haven't much hope of winning.

Ten minutes before the race is due to begin a warning cannon is fired from the Royal Yacht Squadron. This is called the "ten minute gun", and for the next five minutes the competitors size up the wind and weather ready for the start.

At five minutes to go, another gun is fired and this time the Blue Peter flag is hoisted over the Royal Yacht Squadron. When the five minutes are up, there's

another bang—and you're away!

That five minutes before the start is absolute chaos in the harbour. Every captain is trying to get his boat in the best possible position, and no one is giving an inch.

"Races are won and lost on the starting line," declared Christopher, looking anxiously at his watch.

The five minute gun boomed out across the harbour.

"One and a half minutes due east, go about, and we should be about right," he muttered.

We were almost round when the navigator looked up from his stopwatch and rapped: "Two minutes to the start." Facing the wind now, we had to tack across the harbour, weaving in and out of the other competitors and hoping we had got the timing right.

Alan's head emerged from the hatch. "One minute now—fifty-five—fifty," he called as we were bearing down on the line. "Thirty—twenty-five," he continued, reading off the watch.

"Count faster can't you!" shouted Christopher as we got nearer the point of disqualification.

"Five—four—three—two—one!" The bows lifted out of the water as we crossed the line with hardly a second in hand—we were off!

When you are sailing against the wind, huge bow waves crash over the decks as you tack from port to starboard. "Lee oh!" shouted Christopher, and we ducked as the boom swung across and half the English Channel washed over our decks!

"They say that sailing," said Christopher, wrestling with the wheel, "is like tearing up five-pound notes whilst standing under a cold shower," and looking at the £25,000 worth of gleaming ketch and her soaking skipper, I could understand what they meant.

On the return journey, we had a following wind, which meant that we hoisted the spinnaker, a huge coloured sail which billowed out over the bows. I helped by pulling on a rope (called a sheet) as Christopher commanded, which varied the amount of wind caught in the sail.

We came seventh out of sixty-one, which wasn't at all bad, although once we'd got back to Cowes everyone was more interested in the next day's sailing than in the race we'd just finished.

The sun went down over the forest of masts, and soon lights twinkled on the *Britannia* and the floodlights blazed outside the Royal Yacht Squadron. Music began to drift across the water, and the afternoon's hoary skippers and their crews emerged miraculously sleek and elegant from their little boats. The race was over, but the social whirl was only just beginning.

As the yachtsmen attended the formal ball at the Royal Yacht Squadron, and the less formal parties elsewhere, I don't suppose they spared a thought for the Romans, but I found myself thinking of them.

They had come to Vectis nearly two thousand years ago for their summer holidays, and every visitor since, from Queen Victoria and Lord Tennyson to the children watching the donkey at the well at Carisbrooke Castle, has come for exactly the same reason.

Lord Mountbatten told me that people who live on the Isle of Wight, the islanders, call everybody else "Overners"; as long as it offers its visitors so much, the "Overners" will carry on crossing over to the island.

In the same series:
Blue Peter Special Assignment
Hong Kong and Malta

Come with Val to Hong Kong and Malta. Explore the Hong Kong streets and bustling harbour, visit a Chinese family in their sampan and travel to the border with mainland China. On the honey-coloured island of Malta mingle with the crowds at the festival of Siggiewi, and retrace the battles of Malta from the Knights of St John to the Second World War.